THE GREEN BOOK OF FORGIVENESS

Other books by Bashirat Abdulwahab

1. From Pain to Purpose (2017)
2. Help There's A Book in My Head (2019)
3. Dispossessed (2019)

The Green Book Of
FORGIVENESS

Bashirat Abdulwahab

ISBN: 978-978-794-576-6

Cover design: *Abdulsalam Ahmed Ayanleye*

Published in Nigeria by:
Authorpedia Publishers
Words Rhymes & Rhythm Limited

Abuja | Lagos | Ibadan
08169027757, 08060109295
www.authorpedia.net/

Dedication

This book is for the most important people in my life. I know there are days when I drive you up the wall and still don't say *"I am sorry"*. Yet, you let go because you genuinely love me. And knowing this, fuels my soul.

ACKNOWLEDGEMENT

All praise is due to Allah who makes all good things complete.

So many people have helped me on my journey of healing, forgiveness and growth and I do not take this for granted.

I am grateful for the help and support that I get from my vital people. Many thanks to my spouse, Kabiru-Sani Isa-Koto for all the 'ginger' and the boys for their great concern for the book. They would always ask: "mummy, how is your next book coming up?"

To my brothers, Engr. Muhammad Tayyeb Abdulwahab (PhD) and Yusuf Balarabe Abdulwahab, thank you for always having my back. To Adda Zee (Mrs Zainab Mustapha Jaji), thank you for always obliging me and writing a befitting foreword for my book. And my dearest sisters; Sakinat Abdul-Wahab and Fatimah Mohammed Abacha, thank you for being my big sisters, crying and smiling with me as I walk through the storms. And to my correct friends and sisters (you know yourselves), the ones with whom we are constantly seeking the pleasure of God and an abode in Paradise, thank you.

And to the team: Authorpedia, the book cover artist, Abdulsalam Ahmed Ayanleye, the editor, Abdul Wahab Lawal, and everyone that contributed in one way or the other to the success of this book, thank you. May Allah honour you. May your joy be full.

TABLE OF CONTENT

FOREWORD

'Bashirat is a veteran of pain'. This is what Sam Obafemi said when he wrote the foreword of 'Dispossessed' a book by Bashirat. Coach Sam is not wrong in his observation.

I believe one needs to read this to understand the thought behind this book and the life journey of the author.

Bashirat came into my life accidentally. We both suffered loss and speaking with her made my grief journey a little easier and made me accept that when people hurt you, that is a part of your life's story

Now, in this book Bashirat explores what it means to forgive. She gives us permission to move on and leave the weight of not forgiving behind. Coming through different types of hurt and yet finding the courage to forgive is the real revelation. In particular I encourage us all to do the exercises in the chapters and ask ourselves these deep questions in order to free our minds and spirits from the hook of not forgiving those who hurt us. We do not want to walk around with a hook forever.

Bashirat delves into the spiritual perspectives of forgiveness in our most prominent faiths of Islam, Christianity and Judaism. She reminds us that forgiveness is indeed a universal phenomenon and no one religion can claim to propagate it more. We are reminded to do more of it and juxtapose it within our relationship with the existential being that is Our God and Creator.

This book makes me in particular recognise that one is always on a journey. This journey culminates in recognising that forgiveness has an end date. It has benefits. Making the decision to move on through pain gives us purpose and frees us. It makes us recognise that there is extreme power in forgiveness which is not to be confused with reconciliation. Forgiveness enables us to be at our best and thrive. We take back our power once we forgive.

I encourage anyone who comes in contact with this book to read it in their quiet time. It is not a book to be rushed. Be present and exhale when you read it. It is a contemplative book that says, *'see it wasn't so hard to forgive after all'*.

Enjoy.

Zainab Mustapha Jaji
MD SkillTensive Training and Development Company Ltd.
Abuja, Nigeria

INTRODUCTION

For two years, I struggled with guilt, resentment, anger, and unforgiveness. I prayed to God every day to forgive me for my past mistakes for two whole years. And suddenly, one day, I thought to myself: what if God had already forgiven me? In that moment, I knew that I was the one struggling to forgive myself and when I did, everything changed.

In my work as a Life Transition Coach and Grief Recovery Counsellor with people of diverse backgrounds and peculiar life experiences, I have come to know that un-forgiveness is something that many people struggle with thereby slowing down their recovery journey. So, it became important to teach and write about forgiveness often, especially via my online channels. I have hosted webinars and taught various classes on forgiveness. I have even recorded and published several podcast episodes as well but, I felt, writing a small guide that could be accessible to the World would be an amazing thing to do. So, I got to work. And here it is, in your hands.

I hope that you find it beneficial.

Yours truly,

Bashirat Abdulwahab.
28th October, 2022
Abuja, Nigeria, West Africa.

Forgiveness does not change the past, but it does enlarge the future. – Paul Boose

CHAPTER 1

"Forgiveness is not weakness. It takes courage to face and overcome powerful emotions."

– Desmond Tutu

FORGIVENESS

Forgiveness is a conscious and deliberate decision to release feelings of resentment towards a person or group that has harmed or hurt you. According to Dr. Federic Luskin of Stanford University, forgiveness can be defined as the *"peace and understanding that comes from lessening the blame of that which has hurt you, taking your life experience less personally, and seeing the cost of holding a grudge"*.

If you were anything like I was between 2014 and 2017, then you probably have a long list of people to forgive; and most likely a longer list of mistakes and failures to forgive yourself for. Interestingly, I was a part of my list too.

In mid-2014, I struggled to forgive my late husband for something I'd rather not share. He was a good man. He was only human and as they say: to err is human. I was so angry that I barely spoke with him except when necessary. I still fixed the meals and served food on time; we weren't keeping malice but we were close to it. I was a time bomb waiting to explode with rage. But the weight of that anger that I carried for a few days was heavy. I wanted to set us both free but I was deeply hurt. And then, when I finally released it, it came with such huge relief and I felt as if a huge burden had been lifted off me.

When you find yourself unforgiving, it can bring anger, anguish, and discord into your relationships with others and also affect your new experiences in life.

I particularly love the description in the *Unforgiveness Hook Metaphor* by Steven Hayes that goes:

> "The hook is very painful. Wherever you go, so does the hook and so does the offender. The only way you can get off the hook is if you allow the offender off first. The cost of not allowing the offender off the hook is perhaps, a lifetime of unhappiness."

Now the question is, would you rather let the offender off the hook, or would you prefer to drag the offender everywhere you go and suffer for a lifetime? Forgiveness is therefore knowing that the power to release the hook lies with you and eventually making a conscious decision to release it.

However, forgiveness doesn't happen overnight. It is a process. And if you are struggling to forgive someone, you might want to consider asking yourself the following question:

Who is the person that I need to forgive and why?

One of the major reasons many find it hard to forgive is the lack of a reason to do so. When you don't feel the need to forgive, it will be difficult to do so.

My clients tell me things like: "I don't think I can ever bring myself to forgive him". "She betrayed me." "He broke my heart."

When you focus on the person that hurt you and the things that they did or said to you rather than focusing on yourself, then you may struggle to let go. But, when you focus on yourself, and the benefits in it for you, then maybe, you'd find it a bit easier to forgive. You must find a strong why. And the strongest reason I have found is this; to liberate yourself and enjoy peace of mind. Is there anything more amazing than being free and at peace with yourself and others? I guess you echoed: NO!

EXERCISE 1:

Who do you need to forgive and why?

Take a moment to reflect on this question and complete the task in your workbook.

WHY IS FORGIVENESS A STRUGGLE?

There are many reasons you may find it hard to forgive. Some of them are as follows:

1. **Your expectations were betrayed.** This is a struggle for many including myself. We have this bogus expectation of people that when they don't meet up, we feel betrayed and hurt. We say things like: "it shouldn't have been him or her". But the question is, why not him or her? Aren't they just as imperfect as we are? Sometimes, we feel that they

had the intention to hurt us. But this is not always the case. They are just humans and sometimes, they will fall short of our expectations. Although there are scenarios where we have people who are known to constantly default, it is always safer to lower our expectations of people. The lower your expectations, the less likely you are to get hurt.

2. **You fear that the person might hurt you again.** Holding onto a grudge for many feels like a lock that denies the offender entry so they do not have access to hurt them again. But, does this work? What I have personally found is that it doesn't. The more we begrudge a person, the longer we remain hurt.

3. **You are still angry and resentful towards the person.** If you still bear a grudge against someone, chances are that you will struggle to forgive them. When you recognise why you begrudge someone, it becomes easier to make your decision to forgive.

4. **You think the best way to punish them is to refuse to forgive them.** This is so common and I hear a lot of my clients say: "I can never forgive her or I can never forgive him after all he/she has done to me". Oftentimes, they think holding on to the grudge is the best form of revenge, but alas, it is not. It only causes more harm to them and no harm to the offender.

5. **You visit the past event too often.** Do you find yourself blaming your present life on a past incident? Do you catch yourself saying things like if I didn't meet that guy my life would still be perfect? Or my life is like that because my aunt always spanked me or my parents scolded me? These and more are reasons we give to ourselves repeatedly to

keep holding onto resentful feelings. When we choose to forgive them, it makes pursuing our healing much easier.

6. **You feel that it is your right to avenge a loved one that was hurt by an offender:** this one is a trap and many are entrapped in it. There is no logical reason why you should avenge your mother for the way your father treated her, especially if your father did not harm you in the process. If you find yourself hell-bent on hurting someone because of what he/she did to another person, then you have an issue to deal with. If you must be involved in such situations, it should be as a mediator not as an avenger. Avenging situations that have nothing to do with you will only cause you unnecessary heartache.

7. **You feel you are setting the person free while you are still hurt only to realise that you are the prisoner.** And the more you hold on to the hurt, the longer you remain imprisoned.

EXERCISE 2:

Why are you struggling to forgive yourself or someone that hurt you?

I will advise that you reflect on this and write down what comes up in your workbook.

EXERCISE 3:

1. **Make a list of all the people you need to forgive.** Ensure your name is on the list if you're one of them.

2. **What did they do to hurt you?** I don't want you to COLOUR the event; just write it as it is. Perhaps they said unpleasant words to you, or they acted in a way that made you feel bad. Whatever it is, ensure that you write it the way it is and not the way it makes you feel because we are subjective beings, being objective can be tough in certain scenarios, but we can always try.

3. **Now ask yourself, why should I forgive them?**

Complete this task in your workbook.

CHAPTER 2

"Resentment is like drinking poison and waiting for the other person to die."

– Carrie Fisher

RESENTMENT

Do you feel a rush of anger and or rage when you come in contact with someone that hurt you? That is resentment at play. Resentment is a feeling of bitterness towards someone or a situation. Other words for resentment are irritation, displeasure, pique, indignation, and so on. Resentment is a deeply seated emotion that can lead to anger and hatred if left unchecked. In a relationship, friendship, or marriage, resentment can bring about trust issues. When friends, family members, or couples begin to resent themselves, it may lead to the end of the relationship if both parties do nothing to resolve it.

How do you know that you resent other people?

How do you know that you resent your spouse, friend, or even one of your parents?

SIGNS TO LOOK OUT FOR

! **Unresolved Arguments:** Unresolved arguments can be little issues left unsorted and not dealt with for a while. When either of the parties refuses to talk about a challenge or an issue or one is unwilling to have the conversation, this can become a big deal and can even breed resentment.

! **Constant Criticism:** Criticism is when you begin to attack the character of the other person, constantly blaming them for situations and pointing at their flaws and mistakes. When everything they do or say is criticised even when there is no need for it, they may begin to feel unloved. When someone begins to feel unloved, then they may stop putting in efforts in making the relationship work.

! **Rage and Vengefulness:** When you begin to feel the need to get back at someone, chances are that you harbour resentful feelings towards him or her. Retaliation often comes with the feelings of uncontrollable anger also referred to as rage. Some people may lose control of themselves as a result of the fury that they feel towards a person or group of people.

! **Feelings of Regret:** I have heard a handful of women say to me: "I shouldn't have married him". "I shouldn't have gone there". "It was the gravest mistake of my life". "I wish I knew better" and more. When you find yourself feeling unhappy as a result of the outcome of a decision that you made, then that is regret at play. Regret and resentment can be comorbid.

! **Avoidance:** If you would rather sulk it in instead of sit to talk about it, then this is you suppressing unpleasant emotions that could lead to deeply seated resentment and depression.

- **You Feel Unheard or Abandoned:** We currently live in a very noisy world where everyone is trying to say something but only a few people feel genuinely heard. These days, people will rather have conversations with their phones and people they barely know online rather than with the humans in their lives. This makes a lot of people feel unheard and abandoned. It is one of the many reasons why marriages struggle. Human interaction is very important in any form of relationship. Once this part is ignored, there is bound to be trouble because one party might start to lose interest and withdraw.

All of the above signs and unpleasant feelings have a way of prolonging your forgiveness journey. Becoming aware of these feelings, allowing yourself to express them and dealing with them can fast-track your journey through forgiveness.

> **"As smoking is to the lungs, so is resentment to the soul; even one puff is bad for you."**
>
> **— Elizabeth Gilbert**

If holding on to resentment isn't serving you, chances are that it is harming you. Truth is that it can harm you. A few years ago, I read a powerful book by Dr. Don Colbert titled Deadly Emotions. In that book, I read stories of many people who had been diagnosed with terminal illnesses as a result of prolonged and suppressed anger, emotional hurt, resentment and other forms of hurtful and unpleasant emotions. Anger, sorrow, resentment, guilt, regret and depressive moods unattended to and untreated can go on to lead to an excess of the stress hormones in our body which in turn makes us prone to terminal illnesses such as Cancer, Liver Dysfunction, heart diseases and more. It is a long list.

Do you remember that in Chapter 1, I tasked you to find a 'Why'? Yes? Have you found it? If YES, bravo!

The number one reason why you may be struggling with unforgiveness is because you don't have a strong reason to. But finding a strong why can be a bit difficult. One way to ease it is by showing empathy towards the offender.

Now, what is empathy? Empathy is standing from the point of view of the offender and trying to understand why they acted the way that they did. Why did they say the things they said? It is the ability to understand and share the feelings of another person. Could it be that they were also hurt or going through a hard time?

Remember what they say about hurt people? They go on to spill their hurt and insecurities on others. What this means is that they need help too but perhaps, they don't know it yet. However, the way that we feel about other people's actions towards us is majorly a result of how we decode the message. How we decode their message or action is a function of who we are, where we are coming from and our past significant emotional experiences. What does it mean to you? Has someone in your past done something similar? What does your emotional memory dig up? When you change the meaning you give to situations, the way you see the situations change. Empathy is therefore, simply finding a good reason to excuse the offender. So, what excuse will you make for the offender?

Now that you have made a list of the people you need to forgive and why you're deciding to forgive them, I want you to start already.

And I am sure you are wondering; how do I start to forgive?

EXERCISE 5:

1. Make a list of all the people you are struggling to forgive and write their offense against their names.

2. Make sure you start from the most hurting to the least hurting.

3. Now, turn the paper upside down and start analysing objectively from the least hurting to the most hurting. Ask yourself these questions:

   ! Is this worth my peace of mind and overall wellbeing?

   ! How much more do I have to live and why should I live it being miserable because of someone else's action?

4. Probe yourself as much as you can and then allow yourself to write against their names: I forgive you.

5. Now, strike that off and go on to the next name!

6. Complete this task in your workbook

7. Now ask yourself, why should I forgive them?

Complete this task in your workbook.

CHAPTER 3

"To forgive is to set a prisoner free and realise that prisoner was you."

– Lewis B. Smedes

SELF-FORGIVENESS

Self-forgiveness is a deliberate decision to release feelings of regret and guilt that you hold against yourself. Although easier said than done, many people struggle to identify that they need to forgive themselves while more people will rather ruminate over their past mistakes rather than let them go. The reasons are not far-fetched. Chief of which is the fact that most people identify with their mistakes. When mistakes of the past become your identity, you indirectly label yourself as a failure. This unconscious labelling may set you back for a long time. And this setback may manifest especially when you are trying to take action on your big goals. So, your ego repeatedly tells you something like "remember how you messed up the last time?" and this can stop you from pressing further. Becoming aware of those unconscious labelling such as; "I am a failure", "I can't seem to get anything done" among others is the first step to self-forgiveness.

GUILT AND UNFORGIVENESS OF SELF

On Eid-l Fitr day of 2017, I finally got to forgive myself for the many things that I did wrong. Or better still, the guilt that I held against myself for so long. It was a long list. First, I felt guilty for encouraging my late husband to travel to Milan even when he told me he didn't feel like it. Secondly, I felt really guilty. I didn't see my father just before he drew his last breath; all of me was with him, but I couldn't move because I was still in mourning. I felt guilty for so many things and I felt God was not pleased with me.

I asked God to forgive me every day, after every single prayer for about two years. On this fateful day, it happened that something shifted, and I asked myself, is God so cruel as not to forgive me? What if God had already forgiven me?

And the answer I got was YES. Indeed, God is the Most Merciful and the Most Pardoning. It was then that it dawned on me that I was the one yet to forgive myself and the moment I did, all the guilt faded away.

"Nothing is more wretched than the mind of a man conscious of guilt"

— Plautus

"The worst guilt is to accept an unearned guilt"

— Ayn Rand

You are probably asking yourself right now: "How do I forgive myself?" I will show you subsequently.

Guilt is a feeling that can be translated as: "I messed up and I deserve to be punished for my mistake". But the problem is that some people often punish themselves for too long. How long do you have to beat yourself up for a mistake that happened years ago?

Now, let's talk about you.

Do you still feel guilty for a past mistake or failure? Do you feel that you deserve to be punished for a past incident?

This is guilt playing on you.

Here are a few reasons why you may struggle to forgive yourself:

1. You feel that you deserve to punish yourself for past mistakes or failures.

2. You capitalise on the failure and mistakes of the past.

3. You struggle to differentiate between your past mistakes and your person.

4. Your self-worth is at an all-time low.

Regret and Unforgiveness of Self

"Forget regret, or life is yours to miss." – Jonathan Larson

What Is Regret?

Regret is an unpleasant feeling that is associated with wrong decisions or actions. People who feel regret feel they could have chosen or done better especially when the consequences of their actions turn out unfavourable. Regret is an impediment to happiness and can leave you with feelings of shame and or remorse. Do you find yourself constantly blaming yourself for the outcome of your decisions, past or recent? That is regret at play. Regret stops you from looking ahead with optimism and seeking possible solutions while leaving you with the feeling of "had I known"; "I shouldn't have"; "I could have" and more.

"The mistake ninety-nine percent of humanity made, as far as Fats could see, was being ashamed of what they were; lying about it, trying to be somebody else." – J.K. Rowling

What Is Shame?

Shame is a feeling of humiliation that creates deep sorrow and sadness as well as a lack of self-worth. This emotion is known to produce an endless circle of negative thinking, resentment, rage, anger and a feeling of helplessness and hopelessness. Shameful feelings could be a result of rejection, body shaming, emotional/domestic abuse or even verbal assault which ultimately deprives people of emotional freedom and strength.

"Shame is a soul eating emotion."

— Carl Gustav Jung

When left unattended, shame can also manifest as low self-confidence, low self-esteem, compulsive behaviours, eating disorders, alcoholism among others. It is also found to be so powerful that it can affect your mental health. Shame is basically the fear of being disconnected and according to Dr Brown, is why we as humans are here.

According to Dr Brown, there are twelve categories of shame

1. Money and work
2. Family
3. Parenting

4. Motherhood or fatherhood

5. Appearance and body image

6. Mental and physical health

7. Addiction

8. Sex

9. Surviving trauma

10. Being stereotyped or labelled

11. Age

12. Religion

Source: Integrativelifecenter.com

There are so many situations as listed above that may cause a person to feel shame. Some people feel shame when they violate a cultural or religious norm. Others may feel shame due to a physical disability, mental or physical illness, past trauma or a mistake of the past. Most people who experience shame often feel like they are being observed under a microscope because of what they see as being wrong with them. Although many of us have experienced this feeling at some point in our lives, there are many ways to dispel this feeling.

How to Let Go of Guilt, Regret and Shame

These three emotions, although light on the tongue, are deeply rooted in our hearts and bodily organs. When left unchecked, they can lead to depression and other somatic (bodily visible) forms of illnesses. So, it is safe to say that these toxic and damaging emotions are matters of the heart. And like Dr Don Colbert wrote in his book, 'Deadly Emotions', most people don't listen to their hearts, they listen to their brains.

1. Acknowledge Your Emotions

Firstly, you must own up to the feeling of guilt, regret and shame. I need you to acknowledge your fault and take the blame for the part you played while also vindicating yourself for the part that was never your fault. So, the first step is to become aware of the existence of these emotions by making a list of past mistakes and failures that you still blame yourself for and incidents that made you feel humiliated.

2. Cultivate Mindful Living

Cultivating the habit of living from moment to moment is an amazing way to deal with guilt, regret and shame. In my experience coaching and counselling people, I see them either brooding over the past with regret or consumed by guilt and shame. Leaving your past where it belongs and saving yourself from the anxiety of the future is one of the most profound ways to deal with these deadly emotions. This moment, right now, is the best gift that you and I have. We can either make it count or waste it. There are many ways to cultivate the habit of living in the moment and I share some below:

'Mindfulness-distraction' is one of the biggest challenges in this age and time. There are too many things vying for our attention on a moment to moment basis. People no longer know how and when to silence their ego, look away, turn off their mobile devices or television. It is a struggle for so many people

including myself. Recently, I have cut down on television screen time by 90% and it has helped me a great deal. But I am still struggling with my mobile device. I find myself going back to it every 5-10 minutes. Although it has since become my mini mobile office, which is an excuse I give myself to cling to it. It is filled with so many distractions that it reduces my level of productivity during the day. I am sure you can relate that some days you have a long to-do list but all you are doing is jumping from one social media application to another.

I love this definition of mindfulness that I found on mindful.org and it goes:

> "Mindfulness is the basic human ability to be fully present, aware of where we are and what we're doing, and not overly reactive or overwhelmed by what's going on around us."

However, cultivating mindfulness does not mean that you have your thoughts, emotions and actions under control all the time. Honestly, I do not have mine under control 100% of the time. What it simply means is that you know when your mind is wandering and you can easily call it back to the moment; to focus on what matters and make it count.
Here are a few tips for cultivating mindfulness in your life:

- ♥ Do one thing at a time

- ♥ Drink mindfully by taking water in sips while sitting down

- Eat mindfully by savouring every spoon
- Immerse in and connect with nature
- Witness the sun as it rises and set
- Walk barefoot on a greenfield
- Start a small garden and nurture it
- Meditate
- Feel your emotions
- Create something
- Use your hands as often as you can as this makes you a more mindful person
- Play - connect with your inner child often
- Do what you love and love what you do

3. PRACTICE SHAME RESILIENCE

Brene Brown, the proponent of *Shame Resilience Theory*, defines it as the process of moving towards empathy (courage, connection and compassion) when we are experiencing shame and away from shame (fear, blame and disconnection). According to Brown, shame makes people feel isolated, trapped, and powerless. Shame triggers vary by person but the most common have been listed in the 12 categories of shame previously. The goal of shame resilience is to help a person experiencing shame to feel the opposite emotions instead. These include connection, empathy, freedom, and power.

It is common for a person who feels shame but does not recognize it to respond by trying to gain power over others, being aggressive, withdrawing, or keeping secrets. Another typical response is to seek approval and belonging. There are ways to become more resilient to shame. Brené Brown outlined four key elements:

.1.	.2.	.3.	.4.
Recognizing, naming, and understanding our shame triggers.	Identifying external factors that led to the feelings of shame.	Connecting with others to receive and offer empathy.	Speaking about our feelings of shame with others.

4. Practice Self-Compassion

We all want to express love, care and kindness towards the people that we care about but we often forget to do the same for ourselves. Self-compassion is simply accepting who you are, being kind and loving towards yourself regardless of your flaws and past failures; knowing that you're only human and as humans, we are far from perfect. We will fall and stray but we must keep rising.

It is simply telling you:

No matter how many times I have failed or messed up, I love myself regardless.

Self-compassion is not just self-care; it is deeper than that. Self-care is only a component of self-compassion. Self-compassion is the opposite of self-neglect, self-sabotage and negative self-regard. People who struggle to forgive themselves have low opinions about themselves. This is a self-destructive habit. When you become compassionate towards yourself, you can give yourself the basics of care, kindness while ensuring that your cup is full. You don't just listen to your brain; you also listen to your heart.

How do you listen to your heart?

You can achieve this by sitting with your emotions and asking yourself: How do I feel? And, how do I make others feel?

If you have read my book titled *Dispossessed*, you would have learnt about the brain wiring exercise by Jim Warner which I reviewed and shared in that book. It is a pragmatic approach to understanding not just yourself but your heart and body.

This is what you need to do:

EXERCISE 4:

Using an adjective, describe you feel in the following areas of your life:

Mentally • Emotionally • Physically • Spiritually
Relationally • Vocationally • Financially

Forgiveness of self also known as intrapersonal forgiveness is when you make the decision to let go of the self-imposed suffering that occurs as a result of something that you did to yourself or something you regret to have done.

"Firstly, you must acknowledge how you feel. Is it guilt, shame or regret?"

What did you do?

In what ways does it show up and or affect your present life?

What amends can you make right now?

Perhaps you feel upset with yourself and this is very justifiable. But, over time, you realise the feeling of regret, shame or guilt doesn't feel good. This is the time to explore letting go and forgiving yourself. But there is more to do.

Practice compassion towards yourself: I know it may sound tough, but sometimes, we go too hard on ourselves for the many things that are not our fault in the first place. Other times, for situations we had very little control over. This is not to say that we should not be accountable to ourselves, but man, sometimes it helps if we could learn to just cut ourselves some slack. I know it doesn't sound like the language you understand, but do it, because it is doable; fix it, if it is fixable; if it is not fixable, learn from it and move forward, regardless. Self-compassion is simply recognising that you are human -

albeit imperfect, giving yourself the basics of care, kindness, love and respect. It is saying to yourself:

I KNOW I MESSED UP.

I KNOW I FAILED AT THAT PROJECT.

I KNOW I SPOKE HARSHLY TO MY PARTNER.

I KNOW I DIDN'T PUT MY BEST FOOT FORWARD.

I KNOW I COULD HAVE DONE BETTER.

BUT I LOVE MYSELF REGARDLESS.

So, it is safe to say that self-compassion is unconditional kindness, regard and care towards self. It is the absence of self-neglect. Self-compassion also involves the following:

- ♥ Becoming aware of your physical, emotional and mental states and or pain.
- ♥ Treating yourself with kindness and tending to your basic needs because self-care is not selfish.
- ♥ Regarding yourself first because you matter too. Positive self-regard is very important.

- ♥ Being authentic and coming to a place of acceptance of yourself while working on becoming a better version of yourself.

- ♥ Nurturing positive internal dialogue.

- ♥ Keeping your words to yourself. When you say you would do something for yourself, do it. It is called self-respect.

- ♥ Understanding that you are only human and humans are bound to feel this way.

Here is a self-compassion note you can chant (I learnt these words from one of my meditation teachers – Lisa Abramson):

I am having a hard time right now.

Everyone feels this way sometimes.

May I be kind to myself at this moment.

May I give myself the compassion that I need.

You can replace the text above with the words that most describe how you feel right now. It could be:

I am struggling to forgive myself right no

Everyone feels this way sometimes

May I be kind to myself at this moment

May I forgive myself for my past mistakes

May I give myself the compassion that I need.

HOW DO I PRACTISE SELF-COMPASSION?

Practising self-compassion can be very easy. However, many people find it easy to be compassionate towards other people but find it difficult to be compassionate towards themselves. Practising self-compassion can also look like this:

- Listening to your body and giving it what it needs at the right time
- Drinking adequate water
- Getting enough sleep
- Taking some days off work to rest and re-calibrate
- Keeping fit mentally and physically
- Getting a social media detox
- Staying away from toxicity, toxic people and environment
- Eating healthy meals
- Getting that regular medical examination done
- Following through with the Doctor's prescription
- Putting your needs first as against people-pleasing
- Saying NO when the conditions are not self-preserving

- Allowing yourself to let go of hurtful/unpleasant past experiences

Allowing yourself to be present by *"looking past your thoughts so you can drink the pure nectar of this moment"* says Jalaldeen Rumi. Also remember that, as was famously written by Maya Angelou, *"forgiveness is the greatest gift you can give yourself"*.

Whether it's yourself or others, holding on to Unforgiveness is like living in bondage and Forgiveness is the key that will help you set yourself free.

Are there things you feel the need to forgive yourself for?

- Make a list, an all-encompassing one of all the mistakes, failures and issues you need to forgive yourself for.

- Pick one issue and focus on it. This could be a mistake or a failure that did mess you up or someone you wronged.

- Try to identify if there are any limiting beliefs or negative emotions attached to this experience.

- Remember that you may not have power over the situation anymore, but you have the power to respond, react or simply do nothing about it. Bear in mind that you always have a choice.

- Release these negative emotions by being honest and objective about what happened and how it happened. Separating the act from your response can make this easier.

- Accept that it happened.

- Take the next steps to liberate yourself. It could be by apologising to the person you wronged or righting the wrong you did especially if it is something you can correct. You may also want to ask yourself this question: what can I do to right this wrong? However, if it is not a situation to amend, then I'd advise that you just move on with lessons from this mistake and let bygones be bygones.

- Talk yourself out of negative self-talk that may arise as a result of this mistake. Replace these with positive affirmations.

- Now, make a list of your wins including the small ones.

- Celebrate your wins and remind yourself of them often.

Here's why it is so important to forgive yourself and I will write it just as Barbara of Follow Your Own Rhythm wrote it:

"When we forgive ourselves, we energetically say to ourselves even though I made this mistake and even though I'm not perfect, I still love and accept myself.

Of course, you do! Because, self-forgiveness is a path to healing, self-growth, and unconditional self-love." So, please forgive yourself.

Complete the self-forgiveness exercise in the workbook.

CHAPTER 4

SPIRITUAL PERSPECTIVES OF FORGIVENESS

"All religious traditions carry basically the same message, that is, love, compassion and forgiveness. The important thing is that they should be part of our daily lives"

– Dalai Lama

FORGIVENESS IN ISLAM

Forgiveness is an important part of the Islamic religion. As a Muslim, I had struggled with so much guilt and sins that I thought it would take an eternity for Allah to forgive me. But, I am not alone. So many people of similar and differing religious beliefs I have encountered in the course of my work feel the same way.

"Whoever does not show mercy to the people, Allah will not show mercy to him" — Prophet Muhammad (PBUH)

It is safe to say that forgiveness is a universal phenomenon. It is well documented in history across nations. Although, there are great examples in history of how Prophet Muhammad (PBUH) forgave his tribe and the hypocrites that betrayed him and how Jesus did the same for his people; it is shocking to know that many people still struggle to forgive. The main reason is that people often struggle to process the emotions that arise as a result of an unforgiving situation. However, dealing with our emotions is a skill we can all learn and practise over time. When we become more emotionally intelligent, it makes it easier for us to separate the unforgiving situation from our responses and reactions. And as the popular NLP presupposition goes; nothing means anything except the meaning that we give to it. Below is a verse from the Holy Qur'an that drives the point home:

"Hold to forgiveness; command what is right; but turn away from the ignorant." *(Qur'an 7:199)*

"And the retribution for an evil act is an evil one like it, but whoever pardons and makes reconciliation – his reward is [due] from Allah. Indeed, He does not like wrongdoers." *(Quran 42:40)*

Here, we can understand that Allah will reward and bless those who are truly able to forgive. While it may sometimes be the hardest thing we do, we must understand the importance of reconciling with those we may have never thought possible of being forgiven – we must do this if not for ourselves, then at least for Allah.

There are several actions and counsel of the Prophet (PBUH) on forgiveness that are well documented and I reference some of them below.

A'isha, the wife of the Prophet reported Prophet Muhammad (PBUH) as saying, *"When a servant acknowledges his sin and repents, Allah forgives him."* This was narrated by Buhari & Muslim *(curled from Sunnah.com).*

Anas (May Allah be pleased with him) reported:

Messenger of Allah (PBUH) said, "Allah, the Exalted, has said: 'O son of Adam, I forgive you as long as you pray to Me and hope for My forgiveness, whatever sins you have committed. O son of Adam, I do not care if your sins reach the height of heaven, then you ask for my forgiveness, I would forgive you. O son of Adam, if you come to Me with an earth load of sins, and meet Me associating nothing to Me, I would match it with an earth-load of forgiveness." [At-Tirmidhi, who classified it as Hadith Hasan].

Narrated Abu Huraira:

Allah's Messenger (PBUH) said, "The angels keep on asking Allah's forgiveness for anyone of you, as long as he is at his Musalla (praying place) and he does not pass wind (Hadath). They say, 'O Allah! Forgive him, O Allah! be Merciful to him."

Islam teaches that seeking forgiveness is one of the many paths to purifying the soul of a believer and making it free of regret, guilt, shame, anguish and more. The act itself is synonymous to seeking the mercy of Allah.

In Christianity, the phenomenon of forgiveness is not any different from what we find in Islam. Christians are enjoined to forgive one another in the Holy Bible just as we find in the Holy Qur'an. I find this worrisome that although these are revealed in our scriptures, we still find it hard to let go of grievances against one another.

Here are a few apt verses from the Bible:

> "Be kind and compassionate to one another, forgiving each other, just as God forgave you." *(Ephesians 4:32)*
> "For if you forgive other people when they sin against you, your God will also forgive you." *(Matthew 6:14)*
> "Do not judge, and you will not be judged. Do not condemn, and you will not be condemned. Forgive, and you will be forgiven." *(Luke 6:37)*

Kindness and compassion are the foundation of forgiveness. Whether it is intrapersonal, interpersonal or existential, forgiveness cannot occur where the one who has been hurt has not decided to show mercy and compassion. And knowing this is also an attribute of God - the Most Merciful and the Most-Compassionate, says a lot. Imagine God does not show us mercy when we err? Or imagine that we do not have the promise of God to rely on when He has said: if you forgive others, I will forgive you; if you turn to me in repentance, I will accept it. Imagine how miserable our lives will be. I don't even want to imagine it because our flaws are innumerable, yet, our Lord is Oft-Forgiving.

Forgiveness in Other Faiths

In Judaism, forgiveness is also very key. Judaism teaches that because humans have been given free will, they are responsible for their actions. If they commit a wrong action, then they must seek forgiveness. Forgiveness can only be accepted by the victim. (curled from BBC's Bitesize)

Jews place great emphasis on *'teshuva'* or repentance. This is when Jews will actively try to make amends for the wrongs they have committed. They do this by:

1. reflecting on their wrongs
2. seeking forgiveness for their wrongs
3. praying
4. turning to the Torah for guidance

Will God Ever Forgive Me?

Have you ever asked yourself this question: Do you feel a rush of fear and unpleasant emotions when you think of certain sins or mistakes of the past?

I was there too. And for two years, I consistently sought forgiveness from God. Remember I told you how it took me two years to believe that God had forgiven me for my sins and mistakes? And how did I harbour the guilt for two whole years? I thought it would be nice to share tips that could help you do the same. Having engaged in conversations with people of different faiths, it is safe to say that there are three steps to seeking forgiveness.

Through my own experience, I found three amazing ways that work. I gave it a name -The 3Rs of Forgiveness.

R1: Remorse
R2: Repent
R3: Redress

The first step to seeking forgiveness of the Supreme Being is to show remorse. Remorse, simply put, is the feeling of guilt and or regret for an act of wrongdoing. This is usually a result of realising that we are wrong or have committed a sin. To feel remorse is to truly feel sorry for your mistakes or sins. You don't just say "I am sorry"; you feel it.

To repent is to express sincere regret and guilt about an act of wrongdoing. This means that you are aware of your mistake and are ready to take responsibility for your wrongdoing. To complete the process of seeking forgiveness from the Supreme Being, there is one more thing to do - redress.

Redress means to turn a leaf. To refrain from repeating the act of wrongdoing so it doesn't lead to another sin. This will require some discipline and it is not always easy to achieve but it is possible. But, it does not stop there. You must also seek redress. Seeking redress could mean never going back to your old ways. It could mean increasing your good deeds and charitable acts to seek God's pleasure. Whichever path you choose, know that God wants you to turn a new leaf. However, as humans, there is a possibility that we relapse. We sometimes forget. It's okay when you find yourself straying again, what is not okay is forgetting that you need to strive to do the right thing. Don't let guilt set in. Once you find yourself going back to the wrong path, recall yourself and with time, you'd learn not to go back to your old ways.

CHAPTER 5

BENEFITS OF FORGIVENESS

After my most traumatic experiences and having gone far on my healing journey, I realised that forgiveness was an important part of my healing journey. It made moving forward with life easier. At some point, it occurred to me that the resentment, anger, regrets and guilt that I carried with me was harming me. I became miserable because all I did was regurgitate what someone had done to hurt me or the part, they played in compounding my pain and the things they said that hurt just the way the arrow of an archer hits a target.

I felt like I was the target. And for months, I operated from the victim mindset. It felt like everyone was out to hurt me. It was a messy place to be. I am sure you can relate to my ordeal. I would wait for apologies and explanations from my offenders but they never came.

Forgiveness is not the same as reconciliation. It takes two to reconcile. But it takes only one to forgive. It is an act of the will. Forgiveness is not something anyone will sweet talk you into or something that happens by chance. It is an intentional decision. There is nothing automatic about it. Those who eventually forgive are those who choose to release and let go of unpleasant feelings of resentment, anger, shame, regret and guilt. Knowing that this is a choice and you can decide to make that choice right at this moment is vital to your healing process.

I love how Karen Schwartz,M.D of John Hopkins, put it:

"Forgiveness is a choice. You are choosing to offer compassion and empathy to the person who wronged you" instead of offering revenge, hate and bitterness.

So, it is safe to say that forgiveness can occur even when the offender never came back to say:

I am sorry

I know I hurt you deeply

Please forgive me.

Forgiveness can also occur without having to find a personal quality that will redeem the offender. They do not have to turn a new leaf before you choose to forgive them. However, certain relationships require that the party make amends if they wish to remain in it. Marriage is a great example of such relationships. What I have learnt over time is that, if we choose to forgive people based on how worthy of forgiveness they are, then we are bound to imprison ourselves for longer than necessary. It is not about the offender. It is about you; your healing, freedom, joy and peace of mind.

Several research projects on forgiveness have discovered the amazing link between forgiveness and our overall wellbeing. And the connection increases with age - meaning the older you get, the more important it is for you to practise forgiveness. Stanford University's *The Forgiveness Project* confirms this.

Forgiveness is powerful. And the ability to bring you to do so is gracious. When you forgive, it means that you let go of unpleasant emotions such as resentment, anguish, regret and guilt. When these emotions are suppressed within you, they lead to the excess secretion of a stress hormone called cortisol. An excess of this hormone has been found to lead to terminal illnesses such as cancer, heart disease, depression among others. When you release these emotions, you automatically bring down the level of stress hormones secreted in your body. When stress is less, you are positioned to do better in life.

Now you might be thinking, how does forgiving someone who hurt me deeply or even myself benefits me? Below are benefits that you stand to gain:

- **Forgiveness is a spiritual route to God's mercy.** I found that both Islam and Christianity preach that we show people mercy so that we can in turn earn God's mercy. Now, forgiveness is an integral part of being merciful. Mercy, as Wikipedia defines it, is benevolence, forgiveness, and kindness in a variety of ethical, religious, social, and legal contexts. So, let us pause here, who do you need to show some mercy today?

- **Forgiveness removes pain and resentment from your heart.** And when the heart is devoid of pain, anguish or resentment, you become a happier person. Genuinely happy people are those who let go of unpleasant experiences and emotions easily. You cannot hold on to anger, guilt, regret or resentment for too long and expect to enjoy a blissful life. Both states cannot co-exist mutually. And even when they do, one will always take down the other - meaning you can be happy this moment and next moment, you feel very miserable just because you saw or remember something that reminds you of the resentment that you still harbour. You feel like something is stealing your joy away. One of the easiest ways to sustain your happiness and peace of mind is to practise genuine forgiveness and do so often.

- **Forgiveness is linked to a stronger immune system.** When your immune system is strong, then you are less likely to fall ill. Conversely, unforgiveness can weaken your immune system. And when your immune system is weak, you are more likely to fall sick. So again, if you desire to live a vibrant life, then forgiveness is something you might want to consider.

- **Forgiveness can improve your general wellness.** Your overall wellbeing and proneness to ill health or a terminal disease might be largely reduced when you consider forgiving yourself and others more often. When you let go of anger and hostility you reduce your proneness to hypertension and coronary diseases.

- **Forgiveness can reduce your risk of autoimmune disorders.** Doctors find that you are less prone to arthritis, rheumatoid, lupus and auto-immune disorders when you release resentment, bitterness, un-forgiveness and self-hatred.

- **Forgiveness can help you overcome anxiety.** When you finally decide to face and deal with your anxieties, you are indirectly saving yourself from irritable bowel syndrome, panic attacks, and heart palpitations among others.

- **Forgiveness can help you release poisonous anger.** When you choose to release age-long repressed anger over revenge, you are indirectly choosing a life free of incessant headaches, migraines, back pain, depression and even fibromyalgia.

- **Forgiveness can give your relationships a positive boost.** The quality of your relationships might also be linked to forgiveness. Imagine living with a spouse or parent that you despise as a result of the grudge that you bear against them? Have you been there before? Remember in the introductory part of this book, I shared an episode from the past with my late husband. Those few days felt like hell. Sincerely, I do not ever want to be in that situation again. Such a situation when left unattended can slowly turn someone you like into someone you dislike. But, it is easy to draw the line between like and dislike; love and loathe, but when you become indifferent, it can be very dangerous to your relationships. Being indifferent simply means you don't even know how you feel towards the person. However, every relationship that is important to you will cause you pain at some point in time because the people closest to you know your weak points the most; you get to choose if you want to make it work or not by either choosing to forgive and reconcile or not.

- **Forgiveness can help you optimise your self-esteem.** Do you often feel like you don't amount to anything? Shame, guilt, resentment and regret can affect our levels of self-esteem and self-worth in very big ways. Forgiveness, when it comes from a place of compassion, can boost your self-esteem because compassion can manifest as self-respect or the absence of self-neglect. When you let go of these unpleasant emotions, it is a sign that you respect yourself, your body, your emotions and you value your joy and peace of mind. Therefore, the forgiveness of self and others and even the confidence in God's mercy towards us can make us feel more worthy of life, living, joyful relationships, good things and great experiences.

- ♥ **Forgiveness can help you move past your past mistakes.** Do you often find yourself ruminating on a past mistake or a regretful/hurtful experience that you struggle to fall asleep? Inability to forgive can also be linked to insomnia - the inability to sleep. And lack of restful sleep has been linked to a bunch of health issues, such as higher blood sugar levels, liver problems, weight gain and severe depression. Chronic insomnia can also increase the likelihood of some serious diseases and illnesses, including heart attack, stroke among others. Choosing to stay peaceful in the face of frustration ultimately translates into experiencing more restful sleep, a healthier body and more joyful life.

Last Words

I write these last words in hope that this concise guide has been beneficial to you and that as a result of it, someone is forgiven because you have decided to let go.

If there is someone that you truly care about, this book is a worthy gift to give them.

Anger: Appraising Yourself

The Novaco Anger Scale

Assign scores from the number guide/scale below to each of the question that follows. The lowest score, zero, signifies a lack of annoyance while the highest, 5, signifies extreme anger.

0	if you would feel little or no annoyance
1	if you would feel a little irritated
2	if you would feel moderately upset
3	if you would feel quite angry
4	if you would feel very angry

Questions

1. You unpack an appliance that you just bought, plug it in and discover that it doesn't work.

2. Being overcharged by a repairman who helped you out of a bind

3. Being singled out for correction when others go unnoticed

4. Getting your car stuck in the mud or snow

5. You are talking to someone and they don't answer

6. Someone pretends to be something they're not

7. While you are struggling to carry four cups of coffee to your table at the cafeteria, someone bumps into you, spilling the coffee

8. You hung up your coat but someone knocks it to the floor and doesn't pick it up

9. You are hounded by a salesperson from the moment you walk into the store

10. You made plans to go somewhere with a friend who backs out at the last minute leaving you hanging

11. Being joked about or teased

12. You accidentally make a wrong turn in the parking lot. As you get out of your car someone yells at you saying "Where did you learn how to drive"?

13. Your car stalls at a traffic light and the guy behind you keeps blowing his horn

14. You are trying to concentrate but a person near you is tapping their foot

15. Someone makes a mistake and blames it on you

16. You lend someone an important book or tool and they don't return it

17. You have had a busy day, and your roommate or spouse starts complaining about how you forgot to stop at the store

18. You are trying to discuss something important with a friend or relative who isn't giving you a chance to express your feelings

19. You are in a discussion with someone who persists in arguing about a topic they know very little about

20. Someone sticks his/her nose into an argument between you and another person

21. You're already late and the car in front of you is going 25 mph in a 40-mph zone and you can't pass

22. You step on a glob of chewing gum

23. You're mocked by a small group of people as you pass them

24. In a hurry to get somewhere, you tear your favourite pair of pants

25. You use your last quarter to make a phone call, but you are disconnected before you finish dialling and the quarter is not returned

How To Score Yourself:

To determine your score, add up the numbers you wrote in response to the 25 statements. You can interpret your total score according to the following guidelines:

0 – 45: The amount of anger and frustration you generally experience is remarkably low. Only a small percentage of the population will score this low on a test. You might want to examine whether you were honest with your answers and the possibility that you deny angry feelings.

46 – 55: You are substantially more peaceful than the average person.

56 – 75: You respond to life's annoyances with an average amount of anger

76 – 85: You frequently react in an angry way to life's many frustrations. You are substantially more irritable than the average person.

86 – 100: You are plagued by frequent intense furious reactions that do not quickly disappear. You probably harbour negative feelings long after the initial insult has passed. You may experience frequent tension headaches and elevated blood pressure. Your anger may often get out of control and lead to impulsive hostile outbursts, which at times get you into trouble.

- *The Novaco Anger Scale and Provocation Inventory (NAS-PI) was developed by Raymond W. Novaco, PhD.*

Five-Item Guilt Proneness Scale (GP-5)

Instructions:

In this questionnaire, you will read about five situations that people could encounter in day-to-day life, followed by reactions to those situations. As you read each scenario, try to imagine yourself in that situation. Then indicate the likelihood that you would react in the way described below:

1	2	3	4	5
Extremely Unlikely	*Unlikely*	*About 50% Likely*	*Likely*	*Extremely Likely*

1) After realising you have received too much change at a store, you decide to keep it because the salesclerk doesn't notice. What is the likelihood that you would feel uncomfortable about keeping the money?

2) You secretly commit a felony. What is the likelihood that you would feel remorse about breaking the law?

3) At a coworker's housewarming party, you spill red wine on their new cream-coloured carpet. You cover the stain with a chair so that nobody notices your mess. What is the likelihood that you would feel that the way you acted was pathetic?

4) You lie to people but they never find out about it. What is the likelihood that you would feel terrible about the lies you told?

5) Out of frustration, you break the photocopier at work. Nobody is around and you leave without telling anyone. What is the likelihood you would feel bad about the way you acted?

How To Score Yourself:

The scale is scored by averaging the 5 items. Higher scores indicate more guilt-proneness.

- *The five-item guilt-proneness scale (GP-5) was designed by Cohen, T. R., Kim, Y., &Panter, A. T. (2014).*

Reference And Recommended Books

Abdulwahab, B. (2019). Dispossessed: Everything You Need To Know About Loss, Grief, Moving Through and Moving Forward. Abuja Nigeria.

Abdulwahab, B. (2017). From Pain to Purpose. Abuja Nigeria.

Brene, B (2006). Shame Resilience Theory.https://integrativelifecenter.com/

Cohen, T. R., Wolf, S. T., Panter, A. T., & Insko, C. A. (2011). Introducing the GASP scale: A new measure of guilt and shame proneness. Journal of Personality and Social Psychology, 100(5), 947-966. doi: 10.1037/a0022641

Don C., M.D. (2003). Deadly Emotions: Understanding The Mind-BodySpirit Connection That Can Heal or Destroy You. Nashville, Tennessee -USA.

Raymond W. Novaco, PhD.(NAS-PI) Novaco Anger Scale and Provocation Inventory

THE GREEN BOOK OF FORGIVENESS

—•❀✲❀•—

WORKBOOK

CONTENTS

EXERCISE 1: FORGIVING OTHERS

Who do you need to forgive and why? Take a moment to reflect on this question.

EXERCISE 2: FORGIVING YOURSELF

Have you ever thought of why you are struggling to forgive yourself or someone that hurt you? I will advise that you reflect on this and write down what comes up.

EXERCISE 3: THE UNFORGIVENESS BURDEN

Make a list of all the people you need to forgive. And if you're one of them, then ensure your name is on the list.

What did they do to hurt you? Now, I don't want you to COLOUR the event. Just write it as it is. Perhaps they said unpleasant words to you, or they acted in a way that made you feel bad. Whatever it is, ensure that you write it the way it is and not the way it makes you feel.

Now ask yourself, why should I forgive them?

EXERCISE 4: DEALING WITH RESENTMENT

Is there someone that irritates you? What emotions do you feel when you come in contact with the person?

How is holding on to this resentment serving you?

What will happen if you don't release this resentment or thoughts of revenge?

What will happen if you lose control of yourself as a result of rage or suppressed anger?

What will happen if you release these resentful feelings or thoughts of revenge?

EXERCISE 5: NAME AND LET GO

Make a list of all the people you are struggling to forgive:

Write what they have done to you against their names:

Make sure you start from the most hurting to the least hurting.

Now, turn the paper upside down and start analysing from the less hurting.

Ask yourself: Is this worth my peace of mind and overall wellbeing? How much more do I have to live and why should I live it being miserable because of someone else's action?

Probe yourself as much as you can and then allow yourself to write against their names: I forgive you.

EXERCISE 6: ANGER

NOVACO ANGER SCALE

Instructions:

Answer the following questions using the number guide below write:

0	if you would feel little or no annoyance
1	if you would feel a little irritated
2	if you would feel moderately upset
3	if you would feel quite angry
4	if you would feel very angry

Questions

1. You unpack an appliance that you just bought, plug it in and discover that it doesn't work.
2. Being overcharged by a repairman who helped you out of a bind
3. Being singled out for correction when others go unnoticed
4. Getting your car stuck in the mud or snow
5. You are talking to someone and they don't answer
6. Someone pretends to be something you're not
7. While you are struggling to carry four cups of coffee to your table at the cafeteria, someone bumps into you, spilling the coffee

8. You hung up your coat but someone knocks it to the floor and doesn't pick it up
9. You are hounded by salesperson from the moment you walk in the store
10. You made plans to go somewhere with a friend who backs out at the last minute leaving you hanging
11. Being joked about or teased
12. You accidentally make a wrong turn in the parking lot. As you get out of your car someone yells at you saying "Where did you learn how to drive"?
13. Your car stalls at a traffic light and the guy behind you keeps blowing his horn
14. You are trying to concentrate but a person near you is tapping their foot
15. Someone makes a mistake and blames it on you
16. You lend someone an important book or tool and they don't return it
17. You have had a busy day, and your roommate or spouse starts complaining about how you forgot to stop at the store
18. You are trying to discuss something important with a friend or relative who isn't giving you a chance to express your feelings
19. You are in a discussion with someone who persists in arguing about a topic they know very little about

20. Someone sticks his/her nose into an argument between you and another person 21. You're already late and the car in front of you is going 25 mph in 40 mph zone and you can't pass

21. You step on a glob of chewing gum

22. You're mocked by a small group of people as you pass them

23. In a hurry to get somewhere, you tear your favourite pair of pants

24. You use your last quarter to make a phone call, but you are disconnected before you finish dialling and the quarter is not returned

Scoring:

To determine your score, add up the numbers you wrote in response to the 25 statements. You can interpret your total score according to the following guidelines:

0 – 45: The amount of anger and frustration you generally experience is remarkably low. Only a small percentage of the population will score this low on a test. You might want to examine whether you were honest with your answers and the possibility that you deny angry feelings.

46 – 55: You are substantially more peaceful than the average person.

56 – 75: You respond to life's annoyances with an average amount of anger

76 – 85: You frequently react in an angry way to life's many frustrations. You are substantially more irritable than the average person.

86 – 100: You are plagued by frequent intense furious reactions that do not quickly disappear. You probably harbour negative feelings long after the initial insult has passed. You may experience frequent tension headaches and elevated blood pressure. Your anger may often get out of control and lead to impulsive hostile outbursts, which at times get you into trouble.

Reference:

Novaco Anger Scale and Provocation Inventory (NAS-PI) was developed by Raymond W. Novaco, PhD

EXERCISE 7: PROVOCATION

What experience from the past frustrates you?

I feel frustrated by:

--------- ---

Who is the one person(s) you are still angry at?

I am angry at:

What exactly did they do to provoke you?

How did you respond or react to the provocation?

What emotions can you associate with the provocation?

The provocation made me feel:

What was the outcome of your response/reaction?

The unforgiving experience has taught me to:

EXERCISE 8: GUILT & SHAME

FIVE-ITEM GUILT PRONENESS SCALE (GP-5)

Instructions:

In this questionnaire, you will read about five situations that people could encounter in day-to-day life, followed by reactions to those situations. As you read each scenario, try to imagine yourself in that situation. Then indicate the likelihood that you would react in the way described below:

1	2	3	4	5
Extremely Unlikely	*Unlikely*	*About 50% Likely*	*Likely*	*Extremely Likely*

1. After realising you have received too much change at a store, you decide to keep it because the salesclerk doesn't notice. What is the likelihood that you would feel uncomfortable about keeping the money?
2. You secretly commit a felony. What is the likelihood that you would feel remorse about breaking the law?
3. At a co-worker's housewarming party, you spill red wine on their new cream-colored carpet. You cover the stain with a chair so that nobody notices your mess. What is the likelihood that you would feel that the way you acted was pathetic?

4. You lie to people but they never find out about it. What is the likelihood that you would feel terrible about the lies you told?
5. Out of frustration, you break the photocopier at work. Nobody is around and you leave without telling anyone. What is the likelihood you would feel bad about the way you acted?

Scoring:

The scale is scored by averaging the 5 items. Higher scores indicate more guilt proneness.

Reference:

The five-item guilt proneness scale (GP-5) by Cohen, T. R., Kim, Y., & Panter, A. T. (2014).

EXERCISE 9: SELF-FORGIVENESS

What do you struggle to forgive yourself for and why is this a struggle?

Today, I forgive myself for:

In order to move forward, I acknowledge that I was wrong in how I:

I deserve to forgive myself because:

The unforgiving experience has taught me to:

I intend to make amends by:

EXERCISE 10: SEEKING FORGIVENESS FROM GOD

I fear that God will never forgive me for:

I regret the sins I committed because:

I feel remorse for my sins because:

I now sincerely repent by:

In order to seek God's pleasure, I must:

I am deserving of God's mercy because:

I recognise that God is ever merciful because:

I will turn a new leaf by:

About The Author

Bashirat Abdulwahab, MSc. Grief Recovery Counsellor. Serial Author. Crowdfunding Specialist. TEDx Speaker & Life Transition Coach.

Popularly called 'Coach Bashy', Bashirat is a Life Transition Coach, Grief Recovery Counsellor, Author, Corporate Trainer, Administrator and Humanitarian. She is the Lead Coach at The Bashirat Abdulwahab Coaching, a solution and empathy driven life coaching outfit based in Abuja, Nigeria - West Africa.

With over 13 years cumulative experience in humanitarian work, community and women empowerment, skills development, coaching, counselling and training, Bashirat has worked, trained and consulted for organisations like Institute for Media and Society, Lumo Naturals, Learning Impact NG, SOBCA, Foliage Academy, Digibox, Ashake Foundation, Pro-Oratory Limited among others. In addition to the aforementioned, Bashirat has also earned 6 years cognate experience in administrative processes from The National Industrial Court of Nigeria. She has a reservoir of resources that she deploys to help women, young people and organisations harness their potential

As a practising Helping Practitioner, she has carved a niche for herself in grief management and recovery, emotional and mental wellbeing, happiness and forgiveness strategy, inspirational storytelling and self-publishing.

In addition to coaching, counselling, writing and training, Bashirat has harnessed special skills in crowdfunding and has over the years raised millions of Naira for humanitarian causes.

Bashirat is a graduate of the prestigious Bayero University Kano where she bagged B.Sc. and M.Sc. in Mass Communications in 2011 and 2017 respectively. She has over the years acquired certifications in Neuro-Linguistic Programming (NLP Practitioner and Master Practitioner) from The Priority Academy, UK; Diploma in Grief and Bereavement Counselling from KEW Academy, UK; Emotional Intelligence and Mental Health First Aid from SOBCA. She is currently studying Psychology at the International Open University, Gambia. Bashirat is also currently serving as Governor of SOBCA Life Coaches.

Bashirat is a resourceful Speaker, Trainer, Writer and Life Coach. She is a published Author of Bestsellers such as *From Pain To Purpose (2017), Help! There Is A Book In My Head (2019); Dispossessed (2019),* among others. She has featured on various media platforms including Daily Trust Newspaper, Blueprint, Armed Forces Radio, NTA International, Liberty TV & Radio. In 2018, she was named Woman Extraordinaire by Search Inwards Magazine.

Bashirat is married and blessed with two cerebral sons. When she is not working, you would find her spending quality time with her family, writing, exploring and bonding with nature, cycling and drinking tea while reading a good book.

You can contact Coach Bashy via her Website: www.bashiratabdulwahab.com; Instagram/Twitter: @thebashirat; Email: *bashirat.abdulwahab1@gmail.com*, or Call/Text: +234(0)7039599023.

www.ingramcontent.com/pod-product-compliance
Lightning Source LLC
LaVergne TN
LVHW091037150826
845672LV00006BA/1861

* 9 7 8 9 7 8 7 9 4 5 7 6 6 *